A Guy Goes into a Gym

*A Humorous
Dose of Misguided
Makeovers*

ALBERT TAPPER & PETER PRESS

MJF BOOKS
NEW YORK

Published by MJF Books
Fine Communications
322 Eighth Avenue
New York, NY 10001

A Guy Goes into a Gym
LC Control Number 03-115170
ISBN 1-56731-631-X

Manufactured in the United States of America on acid-free paper ∞

MJF Books and the MJF colophon are trademarks of
Fine Creative Media, Inc.

QM   12   11   10   9   8   7   6   5   4   3   2   1

DEDICATIONS

I dedicate this book to Julia Roberts. I don't know Julia and she wouldn't know me if she stepped on me. Nevertheless, I dedicate it to her because, what the hell, you never know.

Albert Tapper

Being a man who considers self-preservation his greatest asset, I dedicate this book to my girlfriend Lorraine, who has lived with me for twelve years, put up with my "mishagas," supported me in the style I have accustomed myself to, and who beautifully prepares our dining table for the Chinese food she orders in every evening. Since I have written three other books and failed to dedicate any of them to her, she is upset. I don't blame her and if she would put down the knife I would be happy to ahhhhhhhh, ahhhhhhhhh . . .

Peter Press

ACKNOWLEDGMENTS

We would like to acknowledge the following people who, in their attempt at helping us achieve a better quality of life, have left us frustrated and disappointed and significantly lowered our self-esteem. Sigmund Freud, Dr. Robert C. Atkins, John Maynard Keynes, Deepak Chopra, and Arnold Schwarzenegger, and all the others who aren't listed but they know who they are! The truth is we are never going to solve most of our neurotic issues, never going to comfortably fit into anything made out of spandex, never going to have our financial assets surpass our inevitable liabilities, never going to meditate into an enhanced state of being, and finally never going to exercise more than once a week on average. There, we said it and we're glad.

A.T. and P.P.

A guy goes into a gym and says to one of the personal trainers, "I'd like to lose some weight by exercising and dieting. Can you help?" The trainer looks at the guy and asks, "How much do you weigh?" The guy says, "I am one hundred pounds overweight." The trainer asks, "What is your normal weight?" The guy says, "Fifty pounds overweight."

Over the years, I have noticed that most two-year-olds are trim. It came to me one day over a cup of black coffee and a carrot that perhaps their diet is the reason. After careful observation of my grandchildren I was able to formulate this new diet.

Breakfast: One scrambled egg, one piece of toast with grape jelly. Eat two bites of egg, using your fingers; dump the rest on the floor. Take one bite of toast then smear the jelly over your face and clothes.

Lunch: Four crayons (any color), a handful of potato chips, and a glass of milk (three sips only, then spill the rest).

Dinner: A rock or an uncooked bean, which should be thrust up your left nostril. Pour iced tea over mashed potatoes; eat with spoon.

A fat man wanted to lose some weight, so he went to a weight loss clinic and asked about their deals. The clinic told him that they had three deals. The first one cost $100, the second one cost $200, and the third one cost $500. Since this man was interested but not desperate to lose weight, he ordered the first deal and gave them $100.

The clinic had the man swim around in a pool and then proceed to the sauna. As he was waiting, a gorgeous blonde entered the sauna. She said, "If you catch me, you can have sex with me!" The man raced around the sauna in an attempt to catch her. However, much to his dismay, he was too slow, so he gave up and went home disheartened. However, he was quite elated after noticing he lost ten pounds. So he went back to the weight loss clinic and asked for their $200 deal.

The clinic happily obliged and had him swim around in the pool, get out, and proceed to the sauna. After waiting several minutes, a gorgeous blonde and a beautiful redhead entered. This time they said, "If you catch one of us, we'll both have sex with you." The fat man chased them with a passion. Unfortunately, they were much too swift for him and he was unable to catch either of them. Again he went home disheartened, but was delighted to discover he had lost twenty pounds. By this time, he was so satisfied with the clinic's weight loss program that he ran back and requested the $500 deal.

Again the clinic happily obliged and had him swim around the same pool, and after swimming for some time, he proceeded to the sauna. With a smile on his face he waited and soon a large, muscular guy walked in and said, "If I catch you, I get to have sex with you!"

A guy decided that he needed to make a New Year's resolution to stop taking life so seriously. He appealed to God with the following prayer:

Grant me the serenity to accept the things I cannot change, and the wisdom to hide the bodies of those I had to kill because they pissed me off. And also, help me to be careful of the toes I step on today, as they may be connected to the ass that I may have to kiss tomorrow. Help me to always give 100 percent at work: 12 percent on Monday, 23 percent on Tuesday, 40 percent on Wednesday, 20 percent on Thursday, 5 percent on Friday. And help me to remember: When I'm having a really bad day and it seems that people are trying to take advantage of me, that it takes forty-two muscles to frown and only four to extend my middle finger.

** Top Ten Reasons Why Diets Are Better Than Sex **

10. You don't have to take off your clothes.
 9. You can go from diet to diet without feeling guilty.
 8. Celery is ALWAYS hard.
 7. On a diet, you carefully consider everything you put in your mouth.
 6. It's GOOD if a diet is over quickly.
 5. Dieting doesn't make you pregnant.
 4. You can doze off in the middle of a diet if you want to.
 3. It's okay if your dog watches.
 2. You can do it with your best friend's husband.

And the number one reason why dieting is better than sex . . .

 1. You don't have to worry if it was good for the cottage cheese too.

Starting January 1, I resolve to:

Let go of my feelings of guilt so I can get in touch with my inner sociopath.

Have the power to channel my imagination into ever-soaring levels of suspicion and paranoia.

Assume full responsibility for my actions, except the ones that are someone else's fault.

No longer need to punish, deceive, or compromise myself, unless, of course, I want to stay employed.

Allow intuition to make up for my lack of good judgment.

Honor my personality flaws, for without them I would have no personality at all.

Not be judgmental at all those censorious, self-righteous people around me.

Not suffer in silence while I can still moan, whimper, and complain.

Learn to trust the universe so I no longer need to carry a gun.

Become aware of my character defects and blame my parents.

Self-Help Bumper Stickers

"My Karma ran over my Dogma!!!"

"Out of body. Back in fifteen minutes!"

"Warning: Dates in calendar are closer than they appear."

"As long as there are tests, there will be prayer in public schools."

"Life is hard. It's breathe, breathe, breathe, all the time."

"Ignore your health and it will go away."

Corporate Zodiac

Astrology tells us about you and your future simply by your birthday. The Chinese Zodiac uses the year of your birth. Demographics tell us what you like, dislike, whom you vote for, what you buy, and what you watch on TV. Well, the Corporate Zodiac goes a step further: simply by your job title, people will have you all figured out . . .

MARKETING: You are ambitious yet stupid. You chose a marketing degree to avoid having to study in college, concentrating instead on drinking and socializing, which is pretty much what your job responsibilities are now. Least compatible with Sales.

SALES: Laziest of all signs, often referred to as "Marketing without a degree," you are also self-centered and paranoid. Unless someone calls you and begs you to take their money, you like to avoid contact with "customers" so you can "concentrate on the big picture." You seek admiration for your golf game throughout your life.

TECHNOLOGY: Unable to control anything in your personal life, you are instead content to completely control everything that happens at your workplace. Often even YOU don't understand what you are saying.

ACCOUNTING: A sign that you studied in school, you are mostly immune from office politics. You are the most feared person in the organization; combined with your extreme organizational traits, the majority of rumors concerning you say that you are completely insane.

HUMAN RESOURCES: Ironically, given your access to confidential information, you tend to be the biggest gossip within the organization. Possibly the only other person that does less work than Marketing, you are unable to return any calls today because you have to get a haircut, have lunch, and mail a letter!

MIDDLE MANAGEMENT: You are completely spineless; you are destined to remain at your current job for the rest of your life. Unable to make a single decision, you tend to measure your worth by the number of meetings you can schedule for yourself. Best suited to marry other Middle Managers, as everyone in your social circle is a Middle Manager.

SENIOR MANAGEMENT: You are catty and cut-throat, yet completely spineless. Unable to make a single decision, you tend to measure your worth by the number of meetings you can schedule for yourself. Best suited to marry other Senior Managers, as everyone in your social circle is a Senior Manager. (Sound familiar?)

CUSTOMER SERVICE: Bright, cheery, positive, you are a fifty-cent cab ride from taking your own life. As a child you asked your parents for a little cubicle for your room and a headset so you could pretend to play "customer service." Continually passed over for promotions, your best bet is to sleep with your boss.

A guy goes into a bookstore and asks the clerk, "Could you tell me where the Self-Help section is?"

The clerk replies, "Don't you think that would defeat the purpose?"

A yogi goes into a pizza parlor and says, "Make me one with everything."

After the yogi got the pizza, he gave the clerk a $20 bill. The clerk pocketed the bill. The yogi said, "Don't I get change?" The clerk said, "Change must come from within."

Have you heard about the dyslexic cow that attained nirvana? It kept on repeating OOOOMMM!

Self-Help Books

PESSIMISM 101
A guy driving reaches a traffic light and it turns red.
He says, "Why me?"

HOSTILITY
A guy goes into a bread line and asks for toast.

SUICIDE
A guy goes into his psychiatrist's office saying he is
feeling suicidal. The therapist says, "It's good to see
you are goal-oriented."

OPTIMISM
A guy goes after Moby-Dick with a rowboat, a har-
poon, and a jar of tartar sauce.

A guy goes into an ashram and meets a friend. He says, "Hi, how are you?"

The other guy replies: "I'm fine, thanks."

"And how's your son? Is he still unemployed?"

"Yes, he is. But he is meditating now."

"Meditating. That's good."

"Well, it's certainly better than sitting around and doing nothing!"

A Guy Goes into a Gym . . .

"**I** think it would be a good idea."
—Mohandas Gandhi when asked what
he thought of Western civilization

Yogaism

"You have the right to remain silent!"

"Don't just do something—Sit there!"

"I wish no gifts, only presence."

A Guy Goes into a Gym . . .

Ten Diet Facts

1. A diet is a weigh of life.
2. The problem with curbing our appetites is that most of us do it at the curb near a fast-food restaurant.
3. The most fattening thing you can put in an ice cream sundae is a spoon.
4. The biggest drawback to fasting for seven days is that it makes one weak.
5. Sweets are the destiny that shapes our ends.
6. Diets are for people who are thick and tired of it.
7. The toughest part of a diet isn't watching what you eat. It's watching what other people eat.
8. A diet is when you have to go to some length to change your width.
9. Most people gain weight by having intimate dinners for two . . . alone.
10. One guideline applies to fat and thin people alike: If you're thin, don't eat fast. If you're fat, don't eat—FAST!

Question: I've heard that cardiovascular exercise can prolong life. Is this true?

Answer: Your heart is only good for so many beats, and that's it. Everything wears out eventually. Speeding up your heart will not make you live longer; that's like saying you can extend the life of your car by driving it faster. Want to live longer? . . . Take a nap.

A guy goes home to visit his folks. His mom asks him to set the table for dinner. He opens the refrigerator and taped to the inside of the door is a risqué picture of a lovely, slender, perfectly built but scantily clad young woman.

"Mom, what's this?" he asks.

"Oh, I put that up there to remind me not to overeat," she answers.

"Is it working?" he asks.

"Yes and no," she explains. "I've lost fifteen pounds, but your dad has gained twenty!"

Thoughts About Exercise

My grandmother started walking five miles a day when she was sixty. She's ninety-seven now, and we don't know where the hell she is.

The only reason I would take up jogging is so that I could hear heavy breathing again.

I joined a health club last year, spent about 400 bucks. Haven't lost a pound. Apparently, you have to show up.

I like long walks, especially when they are taken by people who annoy me.

The advantage of exercising every day is that you die healthier.

If you are going to try cross-country skiing, start with a small country.

Rejected Self-Help Books

1. *Winning through Whining*
2. *Living off Your Parents—Twelve Weeks to Financial Dependency*
3. *Mental Health Isn't for Everyone*
4. *Perspire Away Pounds by Sweating the Small Stuff*
5. *Stop Molesting Your Inner Child*

Sometimes I think no matter how much a guy improves himself, he can't win. . . .

If you put a woman on a pedestal and try to protect her from the rat race . . . you're a male chauvinist.

If you stay at home to do the housework, you're a pansy.

If you work too much, you're avoiding spending time with her.

If you don't work enough, you're a good-for-nothing lazy bum.

If she has a boring repetitive job with low pay, this is exploitation.

If you have a boring repetitive job with low pay, you should get off your ass and find something better.

If she gets a promotion ahead of you, it's equal opportunity.

If you get a promotion ahead of her, that is favoritism.

If you mention how nice she looks, it's sexual harassment.

If you keep quiet, it's male indifference.

If you cry, you're a wimp.

If you don't, you're an insensitive bastard.

If she makes a decision without consulting you, she's a liberated woman.

If you make a decision without consulting her, you're a chauvinist.

If she asks you to do something you don't enjoy, it's a favor.

If you ask her, that's domination.

If you appreciate the female form and frilly underwear, you're a pervert.

If you don't, you're gay.

If you try to keep yourself in shape, you're vain and self-absorbed.

If you don't, you're a slob.

If you buy her flowers, you're after something.

If you don't, you're not thoughtful.

If you're proud of your achievements, you're conceited.

If you're not, you're not ambitious.

A Guy Goes into a Gym . . .

I get enough exercise by stumbling around my house about a mile each day just looking for my eyeglasses and trying, usually with limited success, to locate where I left my watch, checkbook, and wallet.

When you look at some of the people running around in jogging shorts, you begin to question the evolutionary theory of survival of the fittest.

I prefer sit-ups to jumping jacks. At least I get to lie down after each one.

We recently heard about a man who worked out a program of strenuous activities that did not require physical exercise.

1. Beating around the bush
2. Jumping to conclusions
3. Climbing the walls
4. Swallowing his pride
5. Passing the buck
6. Throwing his weight around
7. Dragging his heels
8. Pushing his luck
9. Making mountains out of molehills
10. Hitting the nail on the head
11. Wading through paperwork
12. Bending over backward
13. Jumping on the bandwagon
14. Balancing the books
15. Running around in circles
16. Eating crow
17. Tooting his own horn
18. Climbing the ladder of success
19. Pulling out the stops
20. Adding fuel to the fire

21. Opening a can of worms
22. Putting his foot in his mouth
23. Starting the ball rolling
24. Going over the edge

And after all of this—he picked up the pieces and went home.

For those people getting along in years here is a little secret for building your arm and shoulder muscles—three days a week works well. Begin by
standing outside the house with a five-pound potato
sack in each hand. Extend your arms straight out
from your sides and hold them there as long as you
can until you reach a full minute and then relax.

After a few weeks, move up to ten-pound potato
sacks. After you have mastered the ten-pound sacks
move up to the fifty-pound potato sacks. You should
start feeling stronger. Then move up to a one hundred-
pound potato sack in each hand and again hold your
arms straight for more than a minute.

Next, start adding a couple of potatoes in each of the
sacks.

It is well-documented that for every mile that you jog, you add one minute to your life. This enables you at eighty-five years old to spend an additional five months in a nursing home at $5,000 per month.

Diet Excuses

1. But it was my birthday, so I had to eat the whole cake.
2. If you eat something and no one sees you eat it, it has no calories.
3. If you drink a diet soda with a candy bar, the soda cancels the calories in the candy bar.
4. If you hang around with only fat people, you will look thinner.
5. Chocolate is a vegetable. How, you ask? Chocolate is derived from cacao beans. Bean is a vegetable. Sugar is derived from either sugar CANE or sugar BEETS. Both are plants and plants are vegetables. Thus, chocolate is a vegetable.

Inside me there's a thin person struggling to get out, but I can usually sedate her with four or five cupcakes.

Did you ever see the customers in a health food store? They are pale, skinny people who look half-dead. In a steak house you see robust, ruddy people. Case closed!

One of life's mysteries is how a two-pound box of candy can make you gain five pounds.

Creation Duel

In the beginning God created Heaven and Earth. And the Earth was without form, and void, and darkness was upon the face of the deep. And the Devil said, "It doesn't get any better than this."

And God said, "Let there be light" and there was light. And God said, "Let the Earth bring forth grass, the herb yielding seed, and the fruit tree yielding fruit," and God saw that it was good. And the Devil said, "Drat!"

And God said, "Let us make man in our image, after our likeness, and let him have dominion over the fish of the sea, and over the fowl of the air and over the cattle, and over all the Earth, and over every creeping thing that creepeth upon the Earth." And so God created man in his own image; male and female did He create.

And God looked upon man and woman and saw that they were lean and fit.

And the Devil said, "Not so fast, Yahweh!"

And God populated the Earth with broccoli and cauliflower and spinach, green and yellow vegetables of all kinds, so man and woman would live long and healthy lives.

And the Devil created fast food. And he brought forth the 79-cent double cheeseburger. And the Devil said to man: "You want fries with that?" And man gained five pounds.

And God created the yogurt, that woman might keep her figure that man found so fair. And the Devil brought forth chocolate. And woman gained 5 pounds.

And God said, "Try my crispy fresh salad."

And the Devil brought forth extra-creamy ice cream. And woman gained ten pounds.

And God brought forth running shoes and man resolved to exercise.

And the Devil brought forth remote control so man would not have to toil to change channels. And man gained twenty pounds.

And God brought forth the potato, a vegetable naturally low in fat and brimming with nutrition.

And the Devil created sour cream dip.

And man clutched his remote control and ate the potato swaddled in cholesterol. And the Devil saw and said, "It is good." And man went into cardiac arrest.

And God sighed and created quadruple bypass surgery.

And the Devil canceled man's health insurance.

And woman ventured forth into the land of chocolate and upon returning asked man: "Do I look fat?"

And the Devil said, "Always tell the truth." And man did.

And woman went out from the presence of man and dwelt in the land of Divorce.

Sexual activity may be the best physical exercise to lose weight! Read on:

ACTIVITY	CALORIES BURNED

REMOVING PARTNERS CLOTHES:

With consent...12

Without consent 187

UNHOOKING BRA:

Using two calm hands...7

Using one trembling hand 36

GETTING INTO BED:

Lifting partner 5

Dragging partner along floor 16

PUTTING ON CONDOM:

With erection 1.5

Without erection...300

INSERTING DIAPHRAGM:

If a woman does it 6

If a man does it 680

ORGASM:

Real...27

Faked 160

PENIS ENVY:
For women 3
For men...72
GUILT:
Sex on your lunch hour.......................................2
Putting it on an expense account 3
Enjoying sex despite the
fact that people are starving
in Rwanda...20

Dieter's Vocabulary

Balanced Diet: A cookie in each hand.
Dieting: Breaking the pound barrier.
Destiny: Rich foods shape our ends.
Sandwich Spread: That which you get from eating between meals.
Seafood Diet: When you see food . . . you eat it.
Stressed: The word "stressed" makes perfect sense when you realize that it is "desserts" spelled backward.
Successful Diet: The triumph of mind over platter.

A Guy Goes into a Gym . . .

Somewhat skeptical of his son's newfound determination to become Arnold Schwarzenegger, a father nevertheless followed the teenager over to the weight-lifting department, admiring a set of weights.

"Please, Dad," pleaded the boy, "I promise I'll use 'em every day."

"I don't know, Michael. It's really a commitment on your part," the father pointed out.

"Please, Dad?" the boy continued.

"They're not cheap either," the father came back.

"I'll use 'em Dad, I promise. You'll see."

Finally won over, the father paid for the equipment and headed for the door. From the corner of the store he heard his son exclaim, "What, do you mean I have to carry them to the car!"

A Guy Goes into a Gym . . .

Ten Proverbs for a Healthier Life

1. Age is a very high price to pay for maturity.
2. Going to church doesn't make you a Christian any more than going to a garage makes you a mechanic.
3. My idea of housework is to sweep the room with a glance.
4. Not one shred of evidence supports the notion that life is serious.
5. For every action there is an equal and opposite government program.
6. Bills travel though the mail at twice the speed of checks.
7. Men are from Earth. Women are from Earth. Deal with it.
8. No husband has ever been shot while doing the dishes.
9. Junk is something you've kept for years and throw away three weeks before you need it.
10. In business you are only as smart as your stupidest competitor.

Many people today slide into addictive behavior without realizing it, and as we all know, sleeping is seriously addictive. Just try going a week without sleep. To help with sleeping problems, here's a short test you can take to determine if you are under the influence of Morpheus.

1. Have you ever experienced a loss of memory for events that happened while you were sleeping?
2. Do you ever sleep before noon?
3. Have you ever told yourself, "I can get out of bed any time I want to?"
4. Do you get cranky and irritable after a few days without sleeping?
5. Have you ever spent time on sleeping that you had budgeted for other things?
6. Have you ever had a "short nap" turn into a major binge?
7. Do you ever sleep alone?
8. Do you believe you can't have fun with your friends without sleeping with them?

If you answered "yes" to two or more questions, then do yourself a favor and call 1-800-PETE. Pete, the co-author of this book, has been known to sleep his life away without any serious side effects.

A Guy Goes into a Gym . . .

My wife purchased a week of private lessons for me at the local health club. I called and made reservations with someone named Tanya, who said she is a twenty-six-year-old aerobics instructor. My wife seemed very pleased with how enthusiastic I was to get started. They suggest I keep this "exercise diary" to chart my progress this week.

Day 1
Started the morning at 6:00 A.M. Tough to get up, but worth it when I arrived at the health club and Tanya was waiting for me. She's something of a goddess, with blond hair and a dazzling white smile. She showed me the machines and took my pulse after five minutes on the treadmill. She seemed a little alarmed that it was so high, but I think just standing next to her in that outfit of hers added about ten points. Tanya was very encouraging as I did my sit-ups, though my gut was already aching a little from holding it in the whole time I was talking to her. This is going to be great.

Day 2
Tanya had me lie on my back and push this heavy iron bar up into the air. Then she put weights on it,

for heaven's sake! Legs were a little wobbly on the treadmill, but I made it the full mile. Her smile made it all worth it. Muscles feel great.

Day 3

The only way I can brush my teeth is by laying the toothbrush on the counter and moving my mouth back and forth over it. I believe I have developed a hernia in both pectorals. Tanya was a little impatient with me and said my screaming was bothering the other club members. The treadmill hurt my chest so I tried the rowing machine. Why would anyone invent a machine to simulate an activity rendered obsolete by sails? Tanya told me regular exercise would make me live longer. I don't think I want to live any longer.

Day 4

Tanya was waiting for me with her vampire teeth in a full snarl. I can't help it if I was half an hour late, it took me that long just to tie my shoes. She wanted me to lift dumbbells. Not a chance as the word "dumb" must be in there for a reason. I hid in the men's room until she sent Bruno looking for me.

Day 5

I hate Tanya more than any human being has ever hated any other human being in the history of the world. If there was any part of my body not in extreme pain I would hit her with it. She thought it would be a good idea to work on my triceps. Well, I have news for you, Tanya: I don't have triceps. I used to have triceps, but no longer.

Day 6
Got Tanya's message on my answering machine, wondering where I am. I lacked the strength in my fingers to use the TV remote so I watched eleven straight hours of the weather channel.

Day 7
Well, that's the week. Thank goodness that's over. Maybe next time my wife will give me something a little more fun, like a free root canal.

Seven Least Popular Self-Help Books

1. *Combing! The Revolutionary New Way to Adjust Your Hair*
2. *Men Are from Mars, Women Are from Venus, At Least One Teletubby (per Trademark Association) Is from the West Village*
3. *It's Hopeless* by Jack Kevorkian
4. *A Guide to Arab Democracies* by Osama bin Laden
5. *Brilliant Military Campaigns* by General George Custer
6. *Bob Dole: The Wild Years*
7. *Mike Tyson's Guide to Dating Etiquette*

Six Healthy Ways to Insanity

1. At lunchtime, sit in your parked car with sunglasses on and point a hair dryer at passing cars. See if they slow down.
2. Page yourself over the intercom. Don't disguise your voice.
3. Every time someone asks you to do something, ask if they want fries with that.
4. As often as possible, skip rather than walk.
5. Five days in advance, tell your friends you can't attend their party because you're not in the mood.
6. Tell your children over dinner, "Due to the economy, we are going to have to let one of you go."

A Guy Goes into a Gym . . .

Books on exercise are selling by the thousands. And there's a reason for this: It's a lot easier to read than it is to exercise.

My idea of vigorous exercise is to lift my feet while my wife is vacuuming.

An executive came back from an assertiveness course. It had been suggested that he place a card on his desk to remind him of what he had learned. So he carefully wrote out:

BE DECISIVE

Then he stood back to look at it, considered it, and carefully added a question mark:

BE DECISIVE?

A police car pulls up in front of an old couple's house, and the ninety-year-old husband gets out. The polite policeman explained that the elderly gentleman was lost in the park and couldn't find his way home. "Oh, Morris," said his wife. "You've been going to that park for over thirty years! How could you get lost?" Leaning close to his wife, so that the policeman couldn't hear, Morris whispered, "I wasn't lost. I was just too tired to walk home."

Philosophical Bumper Stickers

1. Seen it all, done it all, can't remember most of it.
2. Hard work has a future payoff. Laziness pays off now.
3. A single fact can ruin a good argument.
4. Some days you're the dog, some days you're the hydrant.
5. The road to success is always under construction.
6. Wrinkles don't hurt.
7. Be careful of your thoughts; they may become words at any moment.
8. Have you ever imagined a world with no hypothetical situations?

A young woman took her troubles to a psychiatrist. "Doctor, you must help me," she pleaded. "It's gotten so that every time I date a nice guy, I end up in bed with him. And then afterward, I feel guilty and depressed for a week."

"I see," nodded the psychiatrist. "And you, no doubt, want me to strengthen your willpower and resolve in this matter."

"For God's sake, NO!" exclaimed the woman. "I want you to fix it so I won't feel guilty and depressed afterward."

A group of bats, hanging from the ceiling of a cave, discover a single bat STANDING upright below them on the floor of the cave. Surprised by this unusual behavior, they ask, "What's wrong with you? What are you doing down there?" The standing bat answers, "*Yoga!*"

In the pursuit of happiness, the hard part is knowing when you've caught it.

Change is inevitable, except from vending machines.

One of the good things about the self-help movement is sometimes you actually get something done:

A man about to go to bed looked out his bedroom window and saw people stealing things from his shed. He called the police, but they told him that no one was in his area, so no one was available to catch the thieves. He said ok, hung up, counted to 30, and rang the police again. "Hello. I just called you a few seconds ago because there were people in my shed. Well, you don't have to worry about them now; I've just shot them all."

Within five minutes there were half a dozen police cars in the area. Of course, they caught the burglars red-handed.

One of the policemen said to the man, "I thought you said you'd shot them!"

He replied, "I thought you said there was no one available!"

Why is it that when we talk to God, we're said to be praying, but when God talks to us, we're schizo-phrenic?

A wife visited a famous psychic. In a dark and gloomy room, gazing at the tarot cards laid out before her, the psychic delivered the bad news:

"There's no easy way to say this, so I'll just be blunt—prepare to become a widow. Your husband will die a violent and horrible death this year."

Visibly shaken, the wife simply had to know. She met the psychic's gaze, steadied her voice, and asked:

"Will I get away with it?"

A Guy Goes into a Gym . . .

"**I** almost had a psychic girlfriend, but she left me before we met."

When two psychic friends met, one said, "You are fine. How am I?"

A young man was walking by a park one day when he saw a softball game in progress. He climbed into the bleachers, sat down, and asked one of the spectators who the teams were.

"The Knights of Columbus are playing the Masons," the spectator replied. "Top of the fourth inning."

"What's the score?" the man asked.

"I don't know," replied the spectator. "It's a secret."

Question: What happens when a Jewish mystic
gets angry?

Answer: He goes Kabalistic.

A frog telephones a psychic hotline and is told, "You are going to meet a beautiful young girl who will want to know everything about you."

"Great," says the frog. "Will I meet her at a party?"

"No, not so great," said the psychic, "You'll meet her in biology class."

A man was married to a psychic. As they were watching TV together on a couch, a sexy commercial came on. It was a beautiful blonde model in a swimsuit trying to sell an exercise tape. The wife poked her husband in the ribs with her elbow. The husband said, "Why did you do that?" The psychic answers, "I know what you were thinking!"

One day a young student at a Buddhist monastery goes to meditate with two monks as part of his education. They go to the opposite side of the lake from the monastery and are about to start their morning meditation when the first monk says, "Oh no, I forgot my mat." So he walks calmly across the surface of the lake to the monastery and returns with his mat. Suddenly the second monk says, "I've forgotten my sun hat." So he runs across the surface of the water to the monastery and returns with his straw hat. This astounds the student and at the end of the meditation he tries to walk across the water. He falls straight in and emerges soaking wet. The two monks are looking on and the first monk says to the second, "Do you think we should have told him where the stones were!"

Why did the Guru refuse novocaine when he went to the dentist? He wanted to transcend dental medication.

A Guy Goes into a Gym . . .

Mr. & Mrs. Smith had just gotten married. On their honeymoon, Mr. Smith said to his new wife, "Would you have married me if my father hadn't left me a fortune?"

She replied, "Darling, I would have married you no matter who left you a fortune."

"You're in great shape," says the doctor. "You're going to live to be eighty."

"But I am eighty," the patient replies.

"So," says the doctor, "did I lie?"

Philosophical Dilemmas

If you try to fail and succeed at it, have you succeeded or failed?

If you listen to a peer telling you not to cave to peer pressure, what have you done?

If it's true that we are here to help others, then what exactly are the others here for?

A visitor from out of town came to tour in Manhattan. At the end of the tour they took him to the financial district. When they arrived at Battery Park the guide showed him some nice yachts anchoring there, and said, "Here are the yachts of our bankers and stockbrokers."

"And where are the yachts of the investors?" asked the naive visitor.

A renowned philosopher was held in high regard by his chauffeur, who listened in awe at every speech while his boss would easily answer questions about morality and ethics.

Then one day the driver approached the philosopher and asked if he was willing to switch roles for the evening's lecture. The philosopher agreed and, for a while, the driver handled himself remarkably well. When it came time for questions from the guests, a woman in the back asked, "Is the epistemological view of the universe still valid in an existentialist world?"

"That is an extremely simple question," he responded. "So simple, in fact, that even my chauffeur could answer that, which is exactly what he will now do."

$\mathbf{A}$ philosophy professor walks in to give his class their final exam. Placing his chair on his desk the professor instructs the class, "Using every applicable thing you've learned in this course, prove to me that this chair DOES NOT EXIST."

So all the students prepare to embark on essays proving that this chair doesn't exist, except for one student. He spends thirty seconds writing his answer and then turns his final in, to the astonishment of his peers.

When all the students get their final grades, to the amazement of the class, the student who wrote for thirty seconds gets the highest grade in the class.

His answer to the question: "What chair?"

A Guy Goes into a Gym . . .

An actuary is walking down the corridor when he feels a twinge in his chest. Immediately, he runs to the stairwell and hurls himself down. His friend, visiting him in the hospital, asks why he did that.

The actuary replies, "The chances of having a heart attack and falling down stairs at the same time are much lower than the chances of having a heart attack only."

A do-it-yourself enthusiast from Arkansas was banned by his wife from taking on any more tasks after causing about $30,000 of damage and leaving a trail of destruction in their two-bedroom terrace house.

While trying to change a washer in the sink, he disconnected two pipes and as a result flooded the house. Later that same day when straightening out the television aerial on the roof, he crashed through the ceiling, showering plaster on his wife as she was ironing.

The very next day he wanted to lay a carpet in the bedroom, but he knocked out the light while bringing the rolled carpet into the house. He then cut a large hole in the carpet rather than move the bed.

If that wasn't enough, in the evening he cut his leg badly when he dropped the drill as he tried to rehang a broken garden gate. Then he drilled through an electric cable, sending out sparks that set fire to the curtains and shut down the electricity.

Then, unable to understand why his electric drill had stopped working, he took it apart to see if he could find the fault. Failing to find anything wrong with it, he tried to put it back together again, but by then he had forgotten where all the pieces went. He went out and bought another drill and was about to take it back because it didn't work, when his wife arrived home and reminded him that he had short-circuited the electricity.

True wisdom comes with age. When you are older you will discover the following:

1. Funny, I don't remember being absentminded . . .
2. If all is not lost, where is it?
3. It is easier to get older than it is to get wiser.
4. The only time the world beats a path to your door is when you're in the bathroom.
5. If God wanted me to touch my toes, he would have put them on my knees.
6. It's not hard to meet expenses . . . they're everywhere.

A woman out for a walk noticed this little old man rocking in a chair on his porch and approached him.

"I couldn't help noticing how happy you look," she said. "What's your secret for a long happy life?"

"I smoke three packs of cigarettes a day," he said. "I also drink a case of whiskey a week, eat fatty foods, and never exercise."

"That's amazing!" the woman said. "How old are you?"

"Twenty-six," he replied.

Approaching eighty-five years of age, Mrs. Harris finally decided it was time to give up her apartment in New York and move to Miami. She was given the name of a Florida realtor, who enthusiastically drove her all over Miami, extolling the virtues of every apartment they looked at.

"And this one, what a steal," he rhapsodized, "the investment of a lifetime. Why, in ten years it's gonna be worth three times . . ."

"Ten years? Sonny," interrupted Mrs. Harris, "at my age I don't even buy green bananas."

It's a relief to know the truth after all those conflicting medical studies:

The Japanese eat very little fat and suffer fewer heart attacks than the British or Americans.

The French eat a lot of fat and also suffer fewer heart attacks than the British or Americans.

The Chinese drink very little red wine and suffer fewer heart attacks than the British or Americans.

The Italians drink excessive amounts of red wine and also suffer fewer heart attacks than the British or Americans.

The Germans drink a lot of beer and eat lots of sausages and fats and suffer fewer heart attacks than the British or Americans.

CONCLUSION: Eat and drink what you like. Speaking English is apparently what kills you.

Self-Help—Label Instructions

On a bag of potato chips:
You could be a winner! No purchase necessary. Details inside.

On frozen dinners:
Serving suggestion: Defrost.

On a hotel-provided shower cap:
Fits one head.

On a cake mix (printed on the bottom of the box):
Do not turn upside down.

On K & L Bread Pudding:
Product will be hot after heating.

On packaging for an electric iron:
Do not iron clothes while on body.

On a sleep aid:
Warning: May cause drowsiness.

On a Korean kitchen knife:
Warning: Keep out of children.

On an airline packet of nuts:
Instructions: Open packet, eat nuts.

For Those Who Take Life Too Seriously

1. A day without sunshine is like night.
2. I wonder how much deeper the ocean would be without sponges.
3. Honk if you love peace and quiet.
4. Despite the cost of living, have you noticed how popular it remains?
5. Atheism is a non-prophet organization.
6. Depression is merely anger without enthusiasm.
7. I intend to live forever—so far so good.
8. Borrow money from a pessimist—they don't expect it back.
9. Never do card tricks for the group you play poker with.
10. The severity of the itch is inversely proportional to the ability to reach it.
11. To succeed in politics, it is often necessary to rise above your principles.
12. Get a new car for your spouse—it'll be a great trade!

Deep Thoughts . . .

LIFE'S OBSERVATIONS

1. Marriage changes passion; suddenly you're in bed with a relative.
2. Sign in a Chinese pet store: "Buy one dog, get one flea."
3. I'm in my own little world. But it's OK, they know me here.
4. Money can't buy happiness, but it sure makes misery easier to live with.
5. If flying is so safe, why do they call the airport the terminal?
6. I don't approve of political jokes. I've seen too many of them get elected.
7. I am a nobody, and nobody is perfect; therefore I am perfect.

Rules of Life

1. You need only two tools: WD-40 and duct tape. If it doesn't move and it should, use WD-40. If it moves and it shouldn't, use the tape.
2. The only really good advice that your mother ever gave you was, "Go! You might meet somebody!"
3. If he/she says that you are too good for him/her . . . believe them.

A Guy Goes into a Gym . . .

Everything You Ever Wanted to Know About Exercise and Diet but Were Afraid to Ask

Question: How can I calculate my body/fat ratio?

Answer: Well, if you have a body, and you have body fat, your ratio is one to one. If you have two bodies, your ratio is two to one, and so on.

Question: Aren't fried foods bad for you?

Answer: Foods are fried these days in vegetable oil. In fact, they're permeated in it. How could getting more vegetables be bad for you?

Question: What's the secret to good healthy eating?

Answer: Thicker gravy.

Question: Will sit-ups help prevent me from getting a little soft around the middle?

Answer: Definitely not! When you exercise a muscle, it gets bigger. So if you do sit-ups you get a bigger stomach.

Question: Is chocolate bad for me?

Answer: Are you crazy? Hello . . . Cacao beans . . . Another vegetable! It's the best feel good food around! (And we already told you that earlier in the book.)

What do you call a vegetarian who goes back to eating meat?

Someone who lost his veg-inity!

The Native American word for *vegetarian* is "poor hunter."

Graffiti on a wall: God is dead! (Signed Friedrich Nietzsche)

Graffiti below that: Friedrich Nietzsche is dead! (Signed God)

While Nostradamus was alive he was in great demand by the temples in the area. Since this got to be a strain running from place to place, the religious groups got their schedules together where they would each get Nostradamus's services for a month on a rotating basis.

It was the world's first prophet-sharing plan.

It Will Pass

A student went to his meditation teacher and said, "My meditation is horrible! I feel so distracted, my legs ache, and I'm constantly falling asleep. It's just horrible!"

"It will pass," the teacher said matter-of-factly.

A week later the student came back to his teacher. "My meditation is wonderful! I feel aware, so peaceful, so alive! It's just wonderful!"

"It will pass," the teacher replied matter-of-factly.

Many students in their search for enlightenment vainly boast that they know nothing, but it is the Guru alone who has truly succeeded in achieving total ignorance.

Mohandas Gandhi was a revered yogi and chose to live a rugged and ascetic lifestyle. He often went barefoot and as a result developed calloused feet. He ate a sparing vegetarian diet including many beans and developed bad breath. He also went on a number of fasts which caused him to become somewhat weak.

He was a "super-calloused fragile mystic with extra halitosis."

Good health is merely the slowest possible rate at which one can die.

Zen Wisdom

1. Do not walk behind me, for I may not lead. Do not walk ahead of me, for I may not follow. Do not walk beside me either. Just leave me the hell alone.
2. The journey of a thousand miles begins with a broken fan belt and a leaky tire.
3. It's always darkest before the dawn. So if you're going to steal your neighbor's newspaper, that's the time to do it.
4. Never test the depth of the water with both feet.
5. If you think nobody cares if you're alive, try missing a couple of car payments.
6. Before you criticize someone, you should walk a mile in their shoes. That way when you criticize them you're a mile away and you have their shoes.
7. If at first you don't succeed, skydiving is not for you.
8. Give a man a fish and he will eat for a day. Teach him to fish and he will sit in a boat and drink beer all day.
9. Timing has an awful lot to do with the outcome of a rain dance.
10. Always remember you're unique—just like everybody else.

The hardest years in life are those between ten and seventy.

—Helen Hayes (at seventy-three)

At my gym they have free weights so I took them home.

A body builder walks into a pizzeria to order a pizza. The waiter asks him, "Should I cut it into six pieces or eight pieces?"

The body builder replies, "I'm feeling rather hungry right now. You'd better cut it into eight pieces."

How All New Year's Resolutions End Up
(We have just chosen a diet to express this.)

Breakfast:

    Half a grapefruit

    1 slice whole wheat toast

    8 oz. skim milk

Lunch:

    4 oz. lean broiled chicken breast

    1 cup steamed spinach

    1 cup herb tea

    1 Oreo cookie

Mid-Afternoon Snack:

    The rest of the cookies in the package

    2 pints chocolate ice cream, nuts, cherries
    and whipped cream

    1 jar hot fudge sauce

Dinner:

    2 loaves of garlic bread

    4 cans or 1 large pitcher of soda

    1 large sausage, mushroom, and cheese pizza

    3 candy bars

Late Evening News:

    Entire frozen cheesecake

Hey—we all start off with good intentions!

A Guy Goes into a Gym . . .

Successfully Proven Facts on Diets

1. When you eat with someone else, calories don't count if you do not eat more than they do.
2. Food used for medicinal purposes NEVER counts. (Examples: hot chocolate, brandy, toast, and cheesecake.)
3. Movie-related foods do not have additional calories because they are part of the entertainment package and not part of one's personal fuel. (Examples: chocolate bars, buttered popcorn, and soda.)
4. Foods that have the same color have the same number of calories. (Examples are: spinach and pistachio ice cream; mushrooms and mashed potatoes; pink grapefruit and ham.)
5. Anything consumed while standing has no calories. This is due to gravity. Isaac Newton proved it centuries ago.
6. Anything consumed from someone else's plate has no calories since the calories rightfully belong to the other person and will CLING to his/her plate.

A Guy Goes into a Gym . . .

Six New Year's Resolutions We Can Keep . . .

1. I want to gain weight, put on at least thirty pounds.
2. Stop exercising. Waste of time.
3. Read less.
4. Watch more TV. I've been missing some good stuff.
5. Spend more time at work.
6. Quit giving money and time to charity.

New Year's Resolutions

January 1 is the date you implement those ever-so-important New Year's resolutions. However, resolutions are difficult to keep. We have faithfully made such resolutions in the past, and while we haven't been able to keep all of them, we have tried our best to continue making progress year after year. We have created a four-year plan that we present for use as a guide:

Resolution #1

Year 1	I will try to be a better husband to Marge.
Year 2	I will not leave Marge.
Year 3	I will try for reconciliation with Marge.
Year 4	I will try to be a better husband to Wanda.

Resolution #2

Year 1	I will not let my boss push me around.
Year 2	I will stick up for my rights when my boss bullies me.

Year 3   I will not let my sadistic boss drive me to the point of suicide.

Year 4   I will tell my therapy group about my boss.

Resolution #3

Year 1   I will read at least twenty good books a year.

Year 2   I will read at least ten books a year.

Year 3   I will read five books a year.

Year 4   I will read the Cliff's Notes.

Resolution #4

Year 1   I will not get upset when Charlie and Sam make jokes about my baldness.

Year 2   I will not get annoyed when Charlie and Sam find out about me and the "HAIR CLUB FOR MEN."

Year 3   I will not get perturbed when Charlie and Sam kid me about my toupee.

Year 4   I will not speak to Charlie and Sam.

Resolution #5

Year 1   I will get my weight down below 180.

Year 2   I will watch my calories until I get below 190.

Year 3   I will follow my diet religiously until I get below 200.

Year 4   When I get below 210 I plan to celebrate.

Resolution #6

Year 1	I will not take a drink before 5:00 P.M.
Year 2	I will not touch the bottle before noon.
Year 3	I will not become a "problem drinker."
Year 4	I will not miss any AA meetings.

Resolution #7

Year 1	I will go to church every Sunday.
Year 2	I will go to church as often as possible.
Year 3	I will set aside time each day for prayer and meditation.
Year 4	I will try to catch the late night sermon on cable.

Useful Wisdom from the East:

Passionate kiss like spider's web, soon lead to undoing of fly.

Foolish man give wife grand piano, wise man give wife upright organ.

Man who walk through airport turnstile sideways going to Bangkok.

Man with one chopstick go hungry.

Man who eat many prunes get good run for money.

Panties not best thing on Earth but next to best thing on Earth.

War doesn't determine who is right, war determines who is left.

Wife who put husband in doghouse soon find him in cathouse.

Eight Things NOT To Do When Applying for a Job

1. Do not challenge the interviewer to an arm wrestle.
2. Do not wear a Walkman and explain that you can listen to the interviewer and the music at the same time.
3. Do not eat a hamburger and fries in the interviewer's office.
4. Do not explain that your long-term goal is to replace the interviewer.
5. Do not say you never finished high school because you were kidnapped and kept in a closet in Mexico.
6. Do not say that to show your loyalty you'll have the corporate logo tattooed on your forearm.
7. Do not phone your therapist for advice on how to answer specific interview questions.
8. Do not bring a large dog to the interview.

You know you're too stressed and need to change your life when:

> You can achieve a "runner's high" by sitting up.
> The sun is too loud.
> You wonder if brewing is really a necessary step for the consumption of coffee.
> You ask the drive-thru attendant if you can get your order to go.
> Antacid tablets become your sole source of nutrition.
> Teddy bears begin to bully you for milk and cookies.

A Guy Goes into a Gym . . .

Six Self-Improvement Courses

1. Overcoming Peace of Mind.
2. How I made $100 in Real Estate.
3. Money Can Make You Rich!
4. Packaging and Selling Your Children.
5. Career Opportunities in Siberia.
6. Inexpensive Lawn Care through Cement.

Planning Your Retirement

After many years at sea, a pirate decided to retire. Since he had suffered injuries on the job, he thought that he should collect on his worker's compensation insurance. He had a wooden leg, a hook where his right hand should be, and a patch over his right eye. The agent assured him that he would be compensated if the injuries were work-related. "How did you get the wooden leg?"

In a booming voice the pirate replied: "Me and me mates were on the high seas when the boom she swang 'round and knocked me into the sea, where a shark bit off me leg."

Agent: "That is certainly work-related. How did you lose your hand?"

Pirate: "Well, matey, me and me mates were on the high seas when the boom she swang 'round and knocked me into the sea, where a shark bit off me hand."

Agent: "That's also work-related. How did you lose your eye?"

In a booming voice the pirate replied: "Well, matey, I was laying on the deck one balmy day catching some rays when this seagull flew by and dropped his duty right in me eye!"

Agent: "What does that have to do with the loss of your eye?"

Pirate: "It were the first day with me hook!"

Airman Jones was assigned to the induction center where he advised new recruits about their government benefits, especially their GI insurance. It wasn't long before Captain Smith noticed that Airman Jones had almost a 100 percent record for insurance sales—that had never happened before. Rather than ask about this, the captain stood in the back of the room and listened to Jones's sales pitch. Jones explained the basics of the GI insurance to the new recruits and then said, "If you have GI insurance and go into battle and are killed, the government has to pay $200,000 to your beneficiaries. If you don't have GI insurance and you go into battle and get killed, the government only has to pay a maximum of $6,000. Now," he concluded, "which bunch do you think they are going to send into battle first?"

The Importance of Planning Ahead

A lawyer and an engineer were fishing in the Caribbean. The lawyer said, "I'm here because my house burned down and everything I owned was destroyed by the fire. The insurance company paid for everything."

"That's quite a coincidence," said the engineer. "I'm here because my house and all my belongings were destroyed by a flood and my insurance company also paid for everything."

The puzzled lawyer asked, "How do you start a flood?"

A Guy Goes into a Gym . . .

A young woman who was worried about her nervous habit of biting her fingernails down to the quick was advised by a friend to take up yoga.

She did, and soon her fingernails were growing normally.

Her friend asked her if yoga had totally cured her nervousness.

"No," she replied, "but now I can reach my toenails so I bite them instead."

A Guy Goes into a Gym . . .

Financial Self-Help for New Investors

Remember the First Law of Economics: For every bullish economist, there is an equal and opposite bearish economist. They are both likely to be wrong! They are both right only 46 percent of the time. A chimpanzee guessing is right 50 percent of the time. Figure that one out!

There are two classes of financial analysts: Those who don't know—and those who don't know they don't know.

October is one of the dangerous months to speculate in stocks. The others are July, January, September, April, November, May, March, June, December, August, and February.

If you want a guarantee, buy a toaster!

A very obese man wants desperately to lose weight so he goes to see a nutritionist. When he walks through the door the nutritionist says, "Wow, I don't mean to be rude, but you are fat!"

The guy says, "Yeah, I know, I'm really fat."

The nutritionist asks, "How long has it been since you've seen your penis?"

The guy says, "Long time."

The nutritionist asks, "Why has it taken you so long to diet?"

The guy asks, "Dye it? Why? What color is it now?"

An author, certain that the royalties on his latest self-help book will be incalculable, interviews for a new accountant. He finds three accountants and interviews them separately.

He calls in the first accountant and asks, "What does two plus two equal?" The accountant replies, "Four." The author asks, "Four, exactly?" The accountant looks at him incredulously and says, "Yes, four, exactly."

Then the author calls in the second accountant and asks the same question, "What do two plus two equal?" The accountant says, "On average, four—give or take ten percent, but on average, four."

Then the author calls in the last accountant and poses the same question to him. "What does two plus two equal?" The accountant gets up, locks the door, closes the shades, sits down next to him, and says, "What do you want it to equal?"

Who do you think the author hired?

This Diet Will Kill 'Ya

Every lunch hour Dave picked up a can of dog food at the grocery store, went across the street to a park bench, and ate the whole can with evident gusto. A doctor who happened to pass through the park regularly couldn't help noticing Dave's behavior and finally decided to offer some advice.

"I'm an internist," he explained, "and I think you should know that dog food isn't a very healthy diet for a human. In fact, eating it could kill you."

"Thanks for the advice, Doc," said Dave, wolfing down another forkful, "but I've been eating it for years now and I feel just fine."

The doctor shrugged and walked off. A few months later he noticed Dave was missing from his bench, so he asked another park regular what had happened.

"He's dead."

The doctor shook his head. "I told him that dog food would kill him."

"It wasn't the dog food that did it," the fellow reported. "He got run over while chasing a car."

To date my wife has lost exactly 2,327 pounds by dieting . . . by my calculations she should now be hanging off the end of a charm bracelet!

I went on a diet and swore off smoking and heavy drinking, and in fourteen days I had lost exactly two weeks.

This year I learned that birth control pills are deductible . . . but only if they don't work.

This year I worked it out carefully. I have all the money I need—as long as I don't buy anything.

This fellow was climbing a tree when suddenly as he reached the top he slipped. He grabbed a branch and was hanging there 75 feet off the ground. He looked up to the heavens and cried out, "God, help me! Please, help me!"

Suddenly the clouds parted and a deep voice resounded, *"Let Go! Trust me! I only help those who help themselves."*

The guy paused and looked up at heaven once more, and said, "I want a second opinion!"

This year I resolve to pay my tax, whereas last year I was lucky if I could just pay attention.

This year I have resolved to use the short form when filing my income tax returns, because then the government gets my money. In the past I have always used the long form, and my accountant got my money.

Cosmetic Surgery

Two women having lunch together were discussing the merits of cosmetic surgery.

The first woman says, "I made a New Year's Resolution. I'm getting a boob job."

The second woman says, "Oh that's nothing. I'm thinking of having my ass reduced!"

To which the first replies, "Whoa, I just can't picture your husband at 5'3"!"

Important Information You Won't Find in Any Self-Help Book

1. The dot over the letter "i" is called a tittle.
2. A raisin dropped in a glass of fresh champagne will bounce up and down continuously from the bottom of the glass to the top.
3. A duck's quack doesn't echo. Pete knows why but he won't tell me.
4. A 2-by-4 really measures 1-1/2-by-3-1/2 inches.
5. During the chariot scene in *Ben Hur,* a small red car can be seen in the distance (and Charlton Heston is wearing a watch).
6. Donald Duck comics were banned from Finland because he doesn't wear pants.
7. There are no words in the dictionary that rhyme with orange, purple, and silver.
8. If one places a tiny amount of liquor on a scorpion, it will instantly go mad and sting itself to death. (Pete was the sadist who discovered this!)

If you've ever had an occasion to visit a gym, you've no doubt heard people talking about "feeling the burn" and "pumping up." But did you ever wonder what people were really saying? Here are some common terms and phrases that will help you to learn what is really going on in the gym:

1. In The Zone—Tired and incoherent during a workout. Commonly referred to as "spaced out."
2. Extended Warm-Up—Twenty minutes at low tension on the stationary bike, then twenty minutes of casual stretching, then a shower.
3. Forced Reps—For the reluctant exerciser, every single rep of a workout is a forced rep. This is especially true when they have a sadistic trainer.
4. Bulking Up—Hamburger before beginning workout.
5. Clean and Press—Surprisingly enough, it's a shoulder exercise, not laundry instructions.

Joey the Dunce's Diet Tips

1. *Eat donuts instead of solid pastries.* You will be saving a tremendous number of calories by eating something with a hole in the middle. You can save upward of three-to-five calories per pastry by doing this. That means if you eat ten donuts, you've saved yourself almost fifty calories! Besides, everyone knows nuts are good for you . . .

2. *French fries can help prevent heart attacks.* It is a fact that French people suffer fewer heart attacks and have lower rates of heart disease. French fries are obviously from France, therefore, it naturally follows that French fries can prevent heart attacks.

3. *Pizza is one of the healthiest foods on the planet.* There are many reasons for this:
    a. The bleached flour in the crust sucks up all the grease that drips down from the toppings.
    b. It's round (stay with me here)—because square-shaped foods have corners, they contain a lot more calories than round foods. To save even more calories, cut a hole in the center of the pizza (refer back to #1 for full details).

c. The cheese on the pizza is loaded with cal-cium—even more than the Tums you're going to need after eating the whole thing.

d. You can easily reduce your servings without sacrificing enjoyment. Instead of cutting the pizza into eight slices, try cutting it into only four. You've just eaten half the number of slices you ate before! Imagine how many calories you'll save by doing that!

e. There is plenty of fiber in the paper that's stuck to the bottom of the pizza. Don't be afraid of it.

4. Beer is the absolute best beverage you can drink when you're watching your waistline. It helps to put it right out there in front of you where you can see it.

A Guy Goes into a Gym . . .

A sweet young thing at a New Year's party turns to her friend and asks for a cigarette.

"I thought you made a New Year's resolution to quit smoking," her friend says.

"I'm in the process of quitting and I'm doing it in two phases. Right now, I'm in the middle of phase one."

"What's phase one?"

"I've quit buying."

Four "New Age" Medications

DAMNITOL
Take two and the rest of the world can go to hell for up to eight hours.

MENICILLIN
Potent antibiotic for older women. Increases resistance to such lines as, "You make me want to be a better person . . . can we get naked now?"

BUYAGRA
Injectable stimulant taken prior to shopping. Increases potency and duration of spending spree.

SEXCEDRIN
More effective than Excedrin in treating the "Not now dear, I have a headache" syndrome.

A Guy Goes into a Gym . . .

Astrologically speaking, how many people does it take to change a lightbulb?

Aries: Just one. You want to make something of it?

Taurus: One, but just "try" to convince them that the burned out bulb is useless and should be thrown away.

Gemini: Two, but the job never gets done—they just keep arguing about who is supposed to do it and how it's supposed to be done!

Cancer: Just one. But it takes a therapist three years to help them through the grief process.

Leo: Leo's done changing lightbulbs, although sometimes his agent will get a Virgo to do the job for him while he's out.

Virgo: Approximately 1,000,000 with an error of + or - 1 millionth.

Libra: Er, two. Or maybe one. No—on second thought, make that two. Is that okay with you?

Scorpio: That information is strictly secret and shared only with the Enlightened Ones in the Star Chamber of the Ancient Hierarchical Order.

Sagittarius: The sun is shining, the day is young, and we've got our whole lives ahead of us, and you're inside worrying about a stupid lightbulb?

Capricorn: I don't waste my time with these childish jokes.

Aquarius: Well, you have to remember that everything is energy, so . . .

Pisces: Lightbulb? What lightbulb?

A woman in our diet club was lamenting that she had gained weight. With her husband away on business, she'd made her family's favorite cake and they'd eaten half of it at dinner.

The next day she said she kept staring at the other half until finally she cut a thin slice for herself. One slice led to another, and soon the whole cake was gone.

The woman went on to tell us how upset she was with her lack of willpower and how she knew her husband would be disappointed. Everyone commiserated until someone asked what her husband said when he returned and found out.

She smiled. "He never found out. I made another cake!"

Pete's Exercise

Pete, the co-author of this book, has his own exercise regime. He has kindly agreed to share it with us. Thank you, Pete.

Pete's idea of exercise is to sit in the tub, pull the plug, and fight the current.

Pete works out every day of the week. His TV remote is broken and getting up out of bed fifty times a night is really tough.

Pete's favorite exercise is running after the Good Humor truck.

Pete is moving into Phase 2 of his exercise program—developing a more aggressive lifestyle. Now he sits and watches aerobic shows on television.

Pete does exercise religiously. He does one sit-up and then says, "Amen."

Pete doesn't want to exercise too rigorously because he doesn't want to feel really stupid lying in a hospital bed some day dying of nothing.

Stress Reduction

Everyone knows stress causes high blood pressure; high blood pressure causes heart attacks; heart attacks cause death. Here's a simple exercise that can add years to your life:

Picture yourself near a stream.

Birds are softly chirping in the crisp cool mountain air.

Nothing can bother you here. No one knows this secret place.

You are in total seclusion from that place called "the world."

The soothing sound of a gentle waterfall fills the air with a cascade of serenity.

The water is clear.

You can easily make out the face of the person whose head you're holding under the water.

It's the person who caused you all this stress in the first place.

What a pleasant surprise. You let them up . . . just for a quick breath . . . then plop! . . . back under they go . . .

There now . . . feeling better?

Marital Counseling Workshop

While attending a marriage seminar on communication, a husband and his wife listened to the instructor declare, "It is essential that husbands and wives know the things that are important to each other."

He addressed the man, "Can you describe your wife's favorite flower?"

The man leaned over, touched his wife's arm gently and whispered, "Pillsbury All-Purpose, isn't it?"

Two confirmed bachelors discussing their New Year's resolutions:

"I think I'll start eating in more often. I got a cookbook," said one.

"It'll never work," said the other.

"What do you mean?" said the first guy.

"Because every recipe starts off 'first find a clean dish,'" said the friend.

Question: What's the difference between an aerobics instructor and a well-mannered
professional torturer?

Answer: The torturer would apologize first.

Question: How many aerobics instructors does it
take to change a lightbulb?

Answer: One! . . . Two! . . . Three! . . .
Four! . . .

Question: What do you call an aerobics instructor who doesn't cause pain and
agony?

Answer: Unemployed.

Financial Self-Help

A man was wondering how to handle his upcoming IRS audit, so he asked his accountant for advice on what to wear. "Wear your shabbiest clothing. Let him think you are a pauper," the accountant replied.

Then he asked his lawyer the same question, but got the opposite advice. "Do not let them intimidate you. Wear your most elegant suit and tie."

Confused, the man went to his rabbi, told him of the conflicting advice, and requested some resolution of the dilemma.

"Let me tell you a story," replied the rabbi. "A woman, about to be married, asked her mother what to wear on her wedding night. 'Wear a heavy, long, flannel nightgown that goes right up to your neck.' But when she asked her best friend, she got this advice, 'Wear your most sexy negligee, with a V-neck right down to your navel.'"

The man protested: "What does all this have to do with my problem with the IRS?"

The rabbi replied, "No matter what you wear, you are going to get screwed."

The best way of saving money is to forget whom you borrowed it from.

Psychotherapist: What seems to be the problem?

Patient: Well, as far as I am concerned, it's my family. You see, I love books and they think that there is something wrong in that; they say that I love them excessively.

Psychotherapist: How ridiculous! They are quite wrong. It is an excellent thing to love books. I love them myself, and always have.

Patient: Oh, it's such a relief to find someone who understands! How do you like them best: boiled or sautéed?

Six Fun New Year's Resolutions

1. Use your MasterCard to pay your Visa and vice-versa.
2. When someone says "Have a nice day," tell them you have other plans.
3. Make a list of things to do that you have already done.
4. Leaf through *National Geographic* and draw underwear on the natives.
5. Stare at people through the tines of a fork and pretend they're in jail.
6. Bill your doctor for time spent in his waiting room.

Seeking and Finding the Truth

While I was watching television, this religious individual showed up on the screen spouting, "Truth, you got to have it. Don't just sit there, don't just stand there, go out there and find Truth!"

I got so excited I couldn't wait. I went straight to the Holy Enlightened One and said, "I got to have Truth. I don't care how big or small it is as long as I know one thing that is true."

The Holy Enlightened One took me out to the country, to a pasture where a farmer grazed his bulls. The Holy Enlightened One said, "Cross this field of bulls and at the other end is a rock. Read what is written on that rock and you will know something that is true."

That pasture was full of fresh cow chips but that wasn't going to stop me. Those cow chips were worse than banana peels. I slipped and fell with each step I took. I was covered with potential fertilizer before I got to that rock of Truth. There was nothing written on it.

Rage went through me in waves. I walked back without slipping or faltering even once. When I got back to where the Holy Enlightened One was standing I screamed at him, "There is nothing written on that rock!"

"Now you know Truth number one," said the Holy Enlightened One.

"You mean I went through all that *&*#!%^&* for nothing?"

"Now you know Truth number two," said the Holy Enlightened One.

I took a couple of showers and soaked in a hot tub filled with rose petal oils before the smell of my experience disappeared. The Holy Enlightened One, seeing me refreshed and dressed, said, "Are you ready for Truth number three?"

I couldn't resist, and took the bait. "What is Truth number three?"

"As you walk through the field of bulls, it matters not how often you slip and fall, or how smeared you get as you search for your own personal Truth, as long as when it is all over you wind up smelling like a rose."

When the government gets finished reforming health care, we might as well stay home and operate on ourselves . . . So I thought we had better learn some medical terminology.

1. Barium—What you do when the patient dies.
2. Urine—The opposite of "You're out!"
3. Cauterize—Made eye contact with her.
4. Ova—Finished; done with.
5. Dilate—To live a long time.
6. Node—Was aware of.
7. Rectum—Danged near killed him.
8. Paradox—Two doctors.
9. Humerus—To tell us what we want to hear.
10. Outpatient—A person that has fainted.
11. Genital—Non-Jew.
12. Pap Smear—To slander your father.
13. Seizure—Roman Emperor.

The Top Three Things You Wish You Could Say to Relieve Stress at Work

1. I can see your point, but I still think you're full of crap.
2. I have plenty of talent and vision. I just don't give a damn.
3. How about "never"? Is "never" good for you?

A Guy Goes into a Gym . . .

Eight Useful Expressions for Those HIGH STRESS Days

1. Well, aren't we just a ray of goddamn sunshine?
2. Not the brightest crayon in the box now, are we?
3. Do I look like a people person?
4. I pretend to work. They pretend to pay me.
5. And your crybaby, whiney-assed opinion would be. . . ?
6. I'm just working here till a good fast-food job opens up.
7. I'm not tense, just terribly, terribly alert.
8. When I want your opinion, I'll give it to you.

In dire need of a beauty makeover, I went to my salon with a fashion magazine photo of a gorgeous young hair model.

I showed the stylist the trendy new cut I wanted and settled into the chair as she began humming a catchy tune and got to work on my thin, graying hair.

I was delighted by her cheerful attitude until I recognized the melody.

It was the theme from "Mission: Impossible!"

A Guy Goes into a Gym . . .

Investing your hard-earned money this year? Here is a glossary of terms that will prove invaluable:

STOCK: A magical piece of paper that is worth $39.95 until the moment you buy it. It will then be worth $37.50!

BOND: What you had with your spouse until you pawned her golf clubs to invest in stocks.

BROKER: The person you trust to help you make major financial decisions. Please note the first five letters of this word spell "Broke."

BEAR: What your wallet will be when you take a flyer on that hot stock tip your masseuse gave you.

BULL: What your broker uses to explain why your mutual funds tanked.

SHORT POSITION: A type of trade where, in theory, a person sells stocks he doesn't actually own. Since this also only ever works in theory, short is really what a person usually ends up being.

COMMISSION: The only reliable way to make money on the stock market, which is why your broker charges you one!

A Guy Goes into a Gym . . .

Relationship self-help books are especially important for married men. Here are some typical complaints from the files of a popular marriage counselor:

- I married Miss Right. I just didn't know her first name was Always.
- It's not true that married men live longer than single men. It only seems longer.
- Losing a wife can be hard. In my case, it was almost impossible.
- A man was complaining to a friend, "I had it all—money, a beautiful house, a big car, the love of a beautiful woman, then pow! It was all gone!" "What happened?" asked the friend. "My wife found out . . ."
- Wife: "Let's go out and have some fun tonight." Husband: "Okay, but if you get home before I do, leave the hallway light on."
- A man rushes into his house and yells to his wife, "Martha, pack up your things! I just won the California lottery!" Martha replies, "Shall I pack for warm weather or cold?" The man responds, "I don't care. Just so long as you're out of the house by noon!"
- Women will never be equal to men until they can walk down the street bald and still think they are beautiful!

If your New Year's resolution was to become more introspective, here are some thoughts for you to consider:

1. If a man is standing in the middle of the forest speaking and there is no woman around to hear him, is he still wrong?
2. If a deaf person swears, does his mother wash his hands with soap?
3. If someone with multiple personalities threatens to kill himself, is it considered a hostage situation?
4. Is there another word for *synonym*?
5. Isn't it a bit unnerving that doctors call what they do "practice"?
6. When sign makers go on strike, is anything written on their signs?
7. Why isn't there mouse-flavored cat food?
8. What do you do when you see an endangered animal eating an endangered plant?

Help for Women Who Want to Get Along with Men

The following are rules men wish women knew:

1. If you think you're fat, you probably are. Don't ask us.
2. Learn to work the toilet seat: If it's up, put it down.
3. Sometimes he's not thinking about you. Live with it.
4. Dogs are better than cats. Period.
5. You have enough clothes.
6. No, he doesn't know what day it is. He never will. Mark anniversaries on a calendar.
7. Yes, peeing while standing up is more difficult than peeing from point blank range. We're bound to miss sometimes.
8. Yes and No are perfectly acceptable answers.
9. A headache that lasts for seventeen months is a problem. See a doctor.
10. Anything we said six or eight months ago is inadmissible in an argument. All comments become null and void after seven days.

A Guy Goes into a Gym . . .

My New Year's Resolution is always to remember to listen to my mom. Why? Because . . .

My mom taught me RELIGION—
"You better pray that will come out of the carpet."

My mom taught me about TIME TRAVEL—
"If you don't straighten up, I'm going to knock you into the middle of next week!"

My mom taught me LOGIC—
"Because I said so, that's why."

My mom taught me FORESIGHT—
"Make sure you wear clean underwear in case you're in an accident."

My mom taught me about CONTORTIONISM—
"Will you look at the dirt on the back of your neck!"

My mom taught me about WEATHER—
"It looks as if a tornado swept through your room."

A Guy Goes into a Gym . . .

My mom taught me about HYPOCRISY—
"If I've told you once, I've told you a million times—
Don't exaggerate!"

My mom taught me THE CIRCLE OF LIFE—
"I brought you into this world and I can take you out."

My mom taught me about BEHAVIOR MODIFICA-
TION—
"Stop acting like your father!"

I finally learned something this year: The difference between tax evasion and taxi evasion. Tax evasion means jail, while taxi evasion means subway.

Improving Your Finances

A study of economics usually reveals that the best time to buy anything is last year.

Money, it turns out, is exactly like sex. You think of nothing else if you don't have it and think of other things if you do.

I hope I don't sound like an old-fashioned stick-in-the-mud, but when I hear about people making vast fortunes without doing any productive work or contributing anything to society, my reaction is: "How can I get in on that?"

Credit cards are VERY dangerous. Every time I try to use one somebody starts chasing me with scissors.

In spite of the cost of living, it's still popular.

The Secret of Success

The other day I had the opportunity to drop by my boss's office. He's a friendly guy and on the rare opportunities that I pay him a visit, we have enjoyable conversations. While I was in his office yesterday, I asked him, "Sir, what is the secret of your success?"

He said, "Two words."

"And, Sir, what are they?"

"Right decisions."

"But how do you make right decisions?"

"One word," he responded.

"And, Sir, what is that?"

"Experience."

"And how do you get experience?"

"Two words."

"And, Sir, what are they?"

"Wrong decisions."

While self-help books sell millions of copies each year, there are twelve things you can only learn from the movies.

1. Large loft apartments in New York City are plentiful and affordable, even if the tenants are unemployed.
2. Should you decide to defuse a bomb, don't worry about which wire to cut. You will always choose the right one.
3. If you are blonde and pretty, it is possible to be a world-famous expert on nuclear fission, dinosaurs, hieroglyphics, or anything else, at age twenty-two.
4. Honest and hard-working policemen are usually gunned down a day or two before retirement.
5. During all crime investigations, it is necessary to visit a strip club at least once.
6. It's easy to land a plane, providing there is someone in the control tower to talk you down.
7. If you are beautiful, your makeup never rubs off, even while scuba diving or fighting aliens. However, if you are overweight, your mascara will run and your lipstick will smear.

8. The ventilation system of any building is the perfect hiding place. No one will ever think to look for you in there and you can travel to any other part of the building without difficulty.

9. You're very likely to survive any battle in any war unless you make the mistake of showing someone a picture of your sweetheart back home.

10. A man will show no pain while taking the most horrific beating, but will wince when a woman tries to clean his wounds.

11. If someone says, "I'll be right back," they won't.

12. A police detective can only solve a case after he has been suspended from duty.

A Guy Goes into a Gym . . .

If you are looking for advice from professionals in diverse fields, it would be helpful to have accurate definitions.

1. An accountant is someone who knows the cost of everything and the value of nothing.
2. An actuary is someone who brings a fake bomb on a plane, because that decreases the chances that there will be another bomb on the plane.
3. An archaeologist is a person whose career lies in ruins.
4. A banker is a fellow who lends you his umbrella when the sun is shining and wants it back the minute it begins to rain.
5. A consultant is someone who takes the watch off your wrist and tells you the time.
6. A diplomat is someone who can tell you to go to hell in such a way that you will look forward to the trip.
7. An economist is an expert who will know tomorrow why the things he predicted yesterday didn't happen today.
8. A lawyer is a person who writes a ten-thousand-word document and calls it a "brief."
9. A sociologist is someone who, when a beautiful woman enters the room and everybody looks at her, looks at everybody.

A Guy Goes into a Gym . . .

One morning a long wed couple were in an amourous embrace and the wife says, "Honey, that Viagra is so wonderful; let me fix us a nice full breakfast . . . eggs, bacon, toast . . ."

The husband says, "No, I'm not hungry. The Viagra takes away my appetite."

Later in the day, the wife says, "Sweetheart, I want to do something for you. Let me fix you a nice wholesome lunch: fresh salad with your favorite ingredients, steamed veggies, and some grilled fish fillets . . ."

The husband again refuses, "Gee honey, I'm just not hungry after using that Viagra."

Around dinnertime, the wife tries again. "Are you hungry yet? I'll fix you steak and potatoes with hot rolls."

The husband still refuses, "No, that Viagra just kills my appetite."

The wife then firmly says, "Well, I'm getting something to eat, so get OFF of me!!!"

Makeover

There was a woman named Candi. She had long, blonde hair and blue eyes, and she was sick of all the blonde jokes. One day she decided to get a makeover, so she cut and dyed her hair. She also went out and bought a new convertible.

With her new car, she went driving down a country road and came across a herd of sheep. She stopped and called the shepherd over.

"That's a nice flock of sheep," she said.

"Well, thank you," said the shepherd.

"Tell you what . . . I have a proposition for you," said the woman.

"Okay," replied the shepherd.

"If I can guess the exact number of sheep in your flock, can I take one home?" asked the woman.

"Sure."

So the girl sat up and looked at the herd for a second and then replied, "382."

"Wow!" said the shepherd. "That's amazing. You're exactly right. Go ahead and pick out the sheep you want to take home." So the woman went and picked one out and put it in her car.

A Guy Goes into a Gym . . .

The shepherd watched this and then said to her, "Okay, now I have a proposition for you."

"What's that?" she asked.

"If I can guess the real color of your hair, can I have my dog back?"

Stress Reduction Chart

1. Attach to firm surface.
2. Follow instructions in step number 4.
3. Repeat until stress is reduced or you become unconscious.

4.
   ```
   BANG
   HEAD
   HERE
   ```

Suicide Help Line

No, no, no. Take the safety OFF first, then pull the trigger.

A Guy Goes into a Gym . . .

American car companies don't have a "help line" for people who don't know how to drive because people don't buy cars the way they buy computers— but imagine if they did . . .

HELPLINE: "American Car Helpline, how can I help you?"

CUSTOMER: "I got in my car and closed the door and nothing happened!"

HELPLINE: "Did you put the key in the ignition and turn it?"

CUSTOMER: "What's an ignition?"

HELPLINE: "It's a starter motor that draws current from your battery and turns over the engine."

CUSTOMER: "Ignition? Motor? Battery? Engine? How come I have to know all of these technical terms just to use my car?"

- - - - - - - -

HELPLINE: "American Car Helpline, how can I help you?"

CUSTOMER: "My car ran fine for a week and now it won't go anywhere!"

HELPLINE: "Is the gas tank empty?"

CUSTOMER: "Huh? How do I know?"

HELPLINE: "There's a little gauge on the front panel with a needle and markings from 'E' to 'F'. Where is the needle pointing?"

CUSTOMER: "I see an 'E' but no 'F'."

HELPLINE: "You see the 'E' and just to the right is the 'F'."

CUSTOMER: "No, just to the right of the 'E' is a 'V'."

HELPLINE: "A 'V'?!"

CUSTOMER: "Yeah, there's a 'C', an 'H', an 'E', then a 'V', followed by 'R', 'O', 'L' . . ."

HELPLINE: "No, no, no, sir! That's the front of the car. When you sit behind the steering wheel, that's the panel I'm talking about."

CUSTOMER: "That steering wheel thingy—is that the round thing that honks the horn?"

HELPLINE: "Yes, among other things."

CUSTOMER: "The needle's pointing to 'E'. What does that mean?"

HELPLINE: "It means that you have to visit a gasoline vendor and purchase some more gasoline. You can install it yourself, or pay the vendor to install it for you."

CUSTOMER: "What? I paid $12,000 for this car! Now you tell me that I have to keep buying more components? I want a car that comes with everything built in!"

- - - - - - - -

HELPLINE: "American Car Helpline, how can I help you?"

CUSTOMER: "Your cars suck!"

HELPLINE: "What's wrong?"

CUSTOMER: "It crashed, that's what went wrong!"

HELPLINE: "What were you doing?"

CUSTOMER: "I wanted to go faster, so I pushed the accelerator pedal all the way to the floor. It worked for a while, and then it crashed—and now it won't even start up!"

HELPLINE: "I'm sorry, sir, but it's your responsibility if you misuse the product."

CUSTOMER: "Misuse it? I was just following this damned manual of yours. It said to make the car go to put the transmission in 'D' and press the accelerator pedal. That's exactly what I did—now the damn thing's crashed."

HELPLINE: "Did you read the entire operator's manual before operating the car, sir?"

CUSTOMER: "What? Of course I did! I told you I did everything the manual said and it didn't work."

HELPLINE: "Didn't you attempt to slow down so you wouldn't crash?"

CUSTOMER: "How do you do that?"

HELPLINE: "You said you read the entire manual, sir. It's on page 14. The pedal next to the accelerator."

CUSTOMER: "Well, I don't have all day to sit around and read this manual you know."

- - - - - - - -

HELPLINE: "American Car Helpline, how can I help you?"

CUSTOMER: "Hi! I just bought my first car and I chose your car because it has automatic transmission, cruise control, power steering, power brakes, and power door locks."

HELPLINE: "Thanks for buying our car. How can I help you?"

CUSTOMER: "How do I work it?"

HELPLINE: "Do you know how to drive?"

CUSTOMER: "Do I know how to what?"

HELPLINE: "Do you know how to DRIVE?"

CUSTOMER: "I am not a technical person! I just want to go places in my car!"

Four Helpful Hints for Everyday Living

1. Never raise your hands to your kids. It leaves your groin unprotected.
2. Always try to be somebody, but try to be more specific.
3. Have you noticed that anyone going slower than you is an idiot, but anyone going faster than you is a maniac?
4. You have six locks on your door, all in a row. When you go out, you lock every other one. No matter how long somebody stands there picking the locks, they are always locking three of them.

Some Handy Hints

1. Save on booze by drinking cold tea instead of whiskey. The morning after, you can still create the effects of a hangover by banging your head repeatedly on the wall.
2. Re-create the fun of a visit to a public swimming pool in your home by filling the bath with cold water, adding two bottles of bleach, then urinating into it, before jumping in.
3. Don't waste money buying expensive binoculars. Simply stand next to the object you wish to view.
4. Olympic athletes: Disguise the fact that you've taken steroids by running a bit slower.
5. Vegetarians coming to dinner? Simply serve them a nice bit of steak or veal. Then ask them how they like the tofu and meat substitute. They'll think it's delicious and say, "Tastes like the real thing."
6. Before attempting to remove stubborn stains from a garment, always circle the stain in permanent pen, so that when you remove the garment from the washing machine you can easily locate the area of the stain and check that it has gone.

7. Heavy smokers: Don't throw away those filters from the end of your cigarettes. Save them up and within a few years you'll have enough to insulate your roof.

8. A mousetrap placed on top of your alarm clock will prevent you from rolling over and going back to sleep.